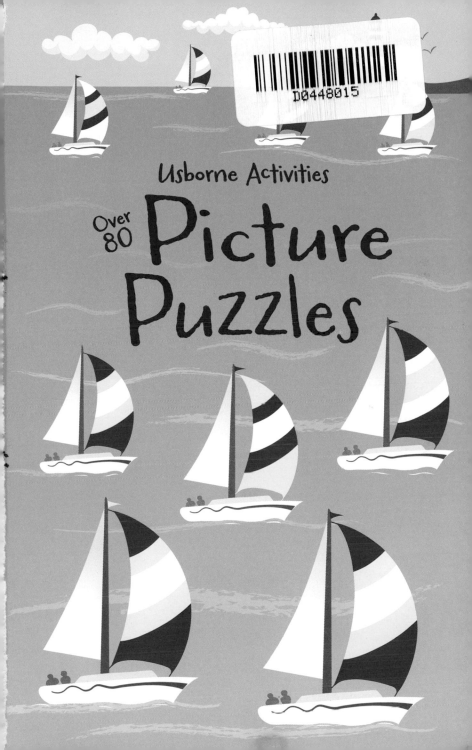

Usborne Activities

Over 80 **Picture Puzzles**

Martian match

Identical twins Zip and Zap are playing outside with their friends. Can you find and circle them?

True or false?

True or false? Underline T or F. In this picture, there are...

1. ...twice as many purple flowers as red ones. T / F

2. ...more butterflies than green frogs. T / F

3. ...no green snakes. T / F

4. ...12 ants. T / F

3

Which map?

Draw a square around the map that represents the scene on the *opposite* page.

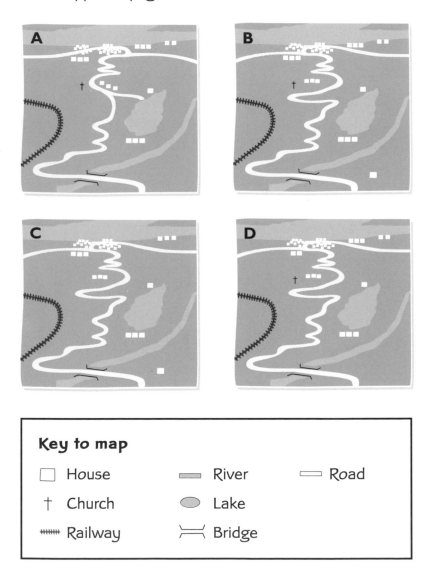

Key to map

☐ House   ▬ River   ▭ Road

† Church   ⬭ Lake

⩗ Railway   ⊢⊣ Bridge

Russian dolls

These Russian dolls come in threes. In each set, the dolls are painted with the same pattern. Circle the doll that isn't part of a set.

Dotty dinosaur

Join the numbered dots in number order, then join the lettered dots in alphabetical order to finish the picture.

Planet maze

Draw a route across the planet to help the astronaut reach the rocket.

Start

Finish

Birdwatching

Look at these birds for one minute, then turn the page. Can you name the bird that has flown away, and is missing from the next page?

Tufted greenwing

Blue bobtail

Songstrel

Long bill

Purple puffling

Golden flufftail

Red breasted pip

Twig wobbler

Birdwatching

Look at the previous page to find out how to do this puzzle.

Answer: ....

Camping count

How many tents are in this scene?

Answer:.................................

Block printing

Circle the two printing blocks that have **not** been used to print this pattern.

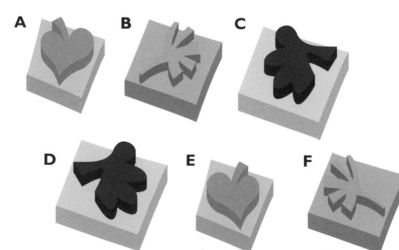

A

B

C

D

E

F

Clothesline

Mrs. Sudds always hangs out her laundry in a particular order. Following that order, can you draw the patterns on the last three socks on the line?

Crocodile crossing

Draw a path across this jungle river, landing only on logs, and avoiding the crocodiles.

Start

Finish

Food symmetry

Food symmetry

Draw lines on each of the plates of food below to show all their lines of symmetry.

Stamp selecting

Using the guide on the opposite page, can you draw lines to connect the correct stamps to each item? You can only use each stamp once.

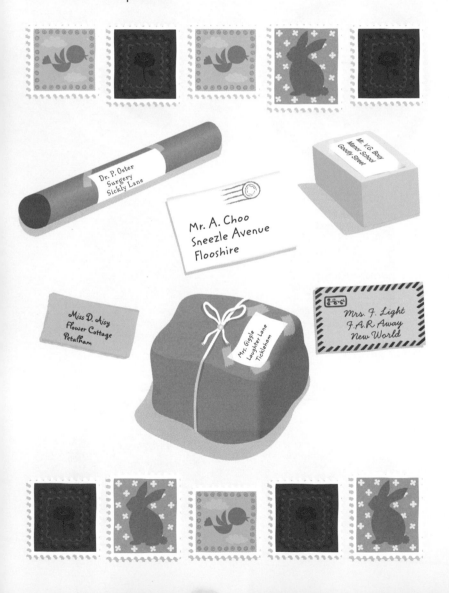

Item	Postage
Small first class letter	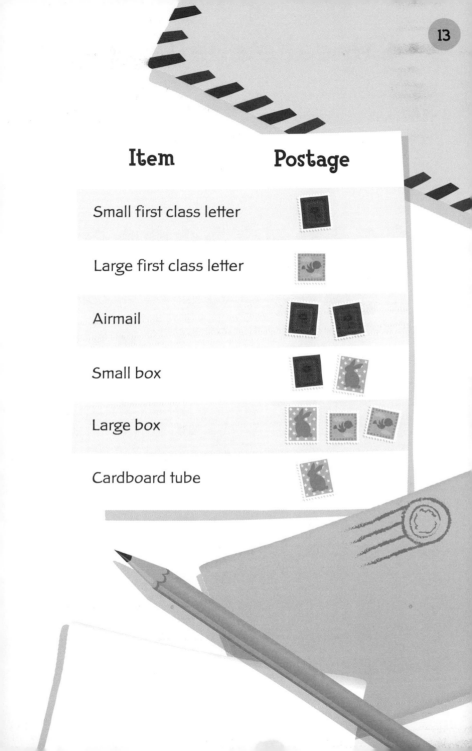
Large first class letter	
Airmail	
Small box	
Large box	
Cardboard tube	

Cupcake challenge

In the picture below,
draw squares around
the groups of cupcakes
that match the groups
shown on the right.

Going bananas

If each of these monkeys eats three bananas, how many bananas will be left on the trees?

Gift wrap

Circle the piece of gift wrap that can be folded to cover the whole box without any overlaps.

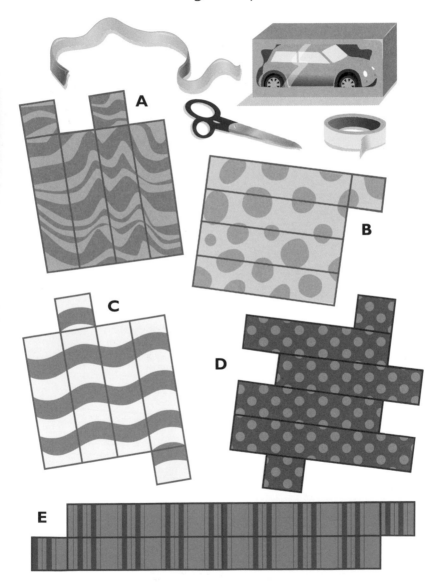

Sailing boats

Circle the two sailing boats that are exactly the same.

Spot the circles

These three circles show parts of the picture below. Can you circle the parts of the picture that match them?

Making masks

1

Here's a list of things that you need to make a tiger mask.
Spend one minute looking at the list, then turn the page
and circle the objects that you **don't** need.

MAKE A TIGER MASK

You will need:
A thin piece of cardboard
A pencil
Scissors
A black marker pen
Orange poster paint
Pink poster paint
A paintbrush
A hole punch
String
Glue

Making masks

Look at the previous page for instructions on how to do this mask-making puzzle.

Robot match

Circle the robots below that match the robot shapes on the right.

Mad scientist's lab

Study this scene, then compare it with the one on the right.

Circle **six** differences in this scene.

Monsters in the dark

Hiding in this dark room is a group of scary, stalk-eyed monsters. Six of them are two-eyed monsters, ten are one-eyed, and the rest are three-eyed. Count the eyes to find out how many three-eyed monsters there are.

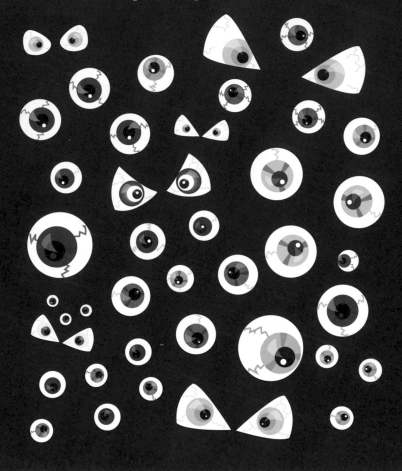

Answer:..

Turning cogs

Draw rings around the two cog arrangements that match each other exactly when one is turned over and rotated.

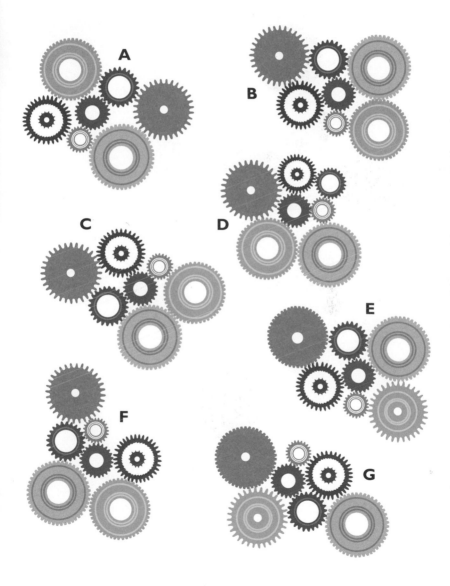

Skewer sequence

Follow the sequence to draw the vegetables onto skewer E in the correct order.

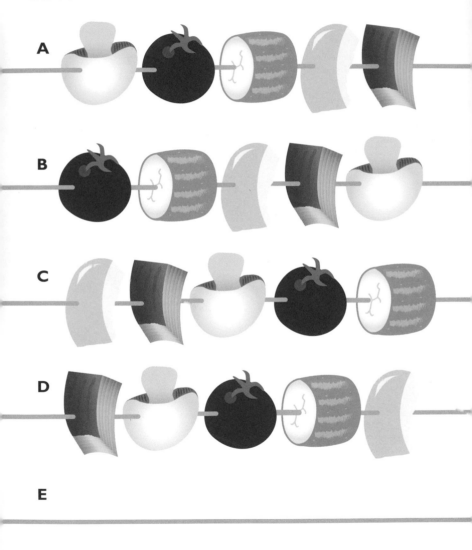

Tower reflection

Draw the mirror image of this half tower to complete the picture.

Curious campsite

Circle the **six** things that are out of place in this summer campsite scene.

Pyramid explorer

Draw a route to the top of the pyramid, using the ladders to go up and down.

Start

Fairground search

Can you find these people in the fairground scene on the right? They're wearing the same clothes, but may not be in the same poses.

Shifting shadows

Draw lines to match each person to their correct shadow.

Musical jumble

How many **different** musical instruments can you find in this jumbled up picture?

Hidden picture

Fill in the shapes that have blue dots. What can you see?

Snail trails

Follow the trails, and circle the snail that has munched on a cabbage.

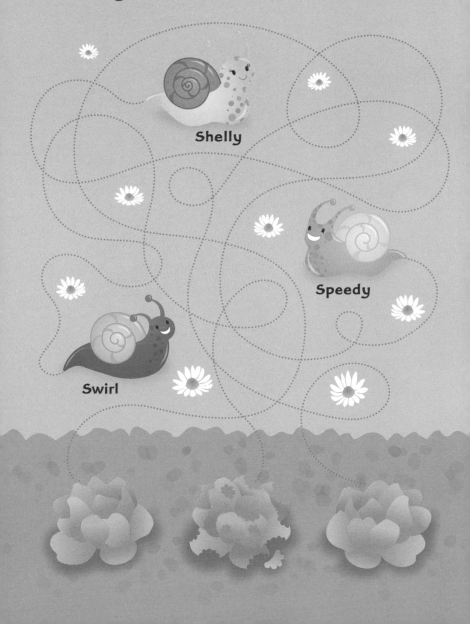

Shadowy waters

Study these fish, then look at the shadows on the opposite page.

1

2

3

4

5

6

7

8

9

10

11

12

13

14

15

Match the shadows to the fish. Write the correct number next to each letter.

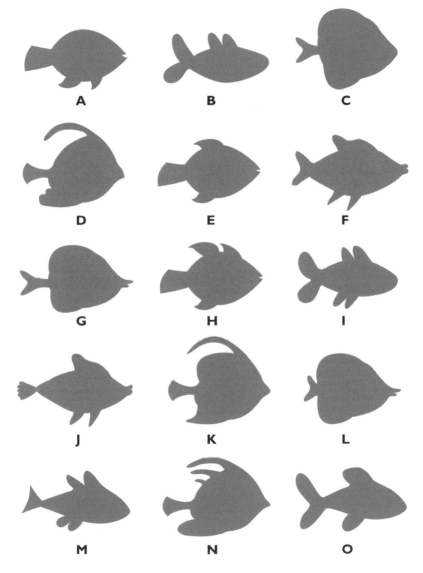

Robot reflection

Draw the mirror image of this half robot to complete the picture.

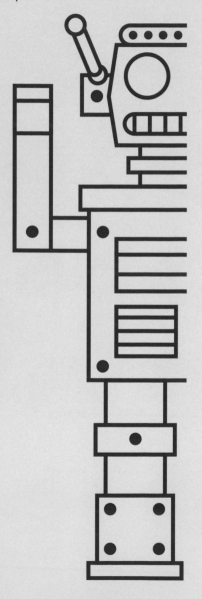

Medieval mistake

Circle the **six** things that didn't exist in Medieval times.

Matching sets

If a set is made up of a matching knife, fork and spoon, how many sets are in this picture?

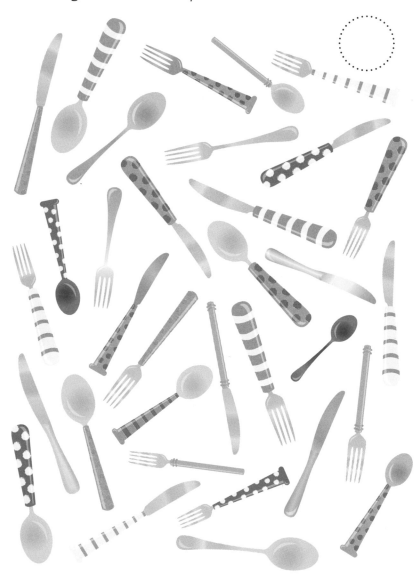

Shape search

How many four-sided shapes can you find in the picture below?

Answer: ....

Something strange

There's something peculiar about each of these pictures.
Draw around the things that seem strange.

The right tools

Joe is going to the hardware store. Memorize this list of tools he needs for 30 seconds, then turn the page to see the things he buys. What has he forgotten?

Things I need...

Wood
Tape measure
Saw
Hammer
Screws
Screwdriver
Wrench
Electric drill
Nails
Paint
Paintbrush

39

The right tools

Look at the previous page to see how to do this puzzle.

Answer:...

Picture match

Circle the picture that **isn't** one of a matching pair.

Monster mirror

Study this picture, then compare it with the reflections on the right.

Circle the picture that shows the correct reflection of the monster.

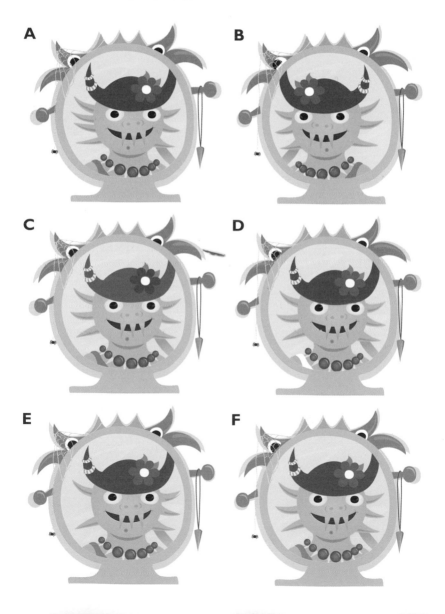

A

B

C

D

E

F

Alien jigsaw

Circle the two pieces that will finish this jigsaw puzzle.

A

B

C

D

Odd one out

Circle the *odd one out* in each row.

1.

2.

3.

4.

Truck parts

Circle the group of parts that can be put together to make up the truck shown on the right.

A
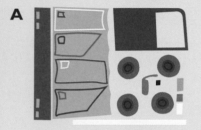

B

C
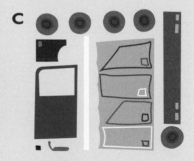

D
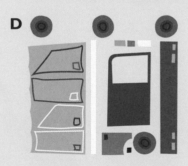

E
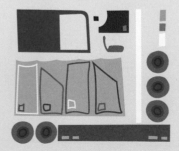

F
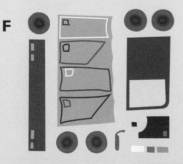

Switching seats

Spend one minute looking at this scene. Then, turn the page and draw Xs on the people who have changed seats.

Switching seats

Look at the previous page to find out how to do this puzzle.

Naughty Kittens

These mischievous kittens have been playing with balls of string and have tangled them up. Follow the trails to find out which kitten is playing with which ball, then write the number of their ball under their names.

Patch

• • • • • • • • • •

1

2

Misty

• • • • • • • • • •

3

Leo

• • • • • • • • • •

Complete the cube

Circle the small cube that completes the large cube.

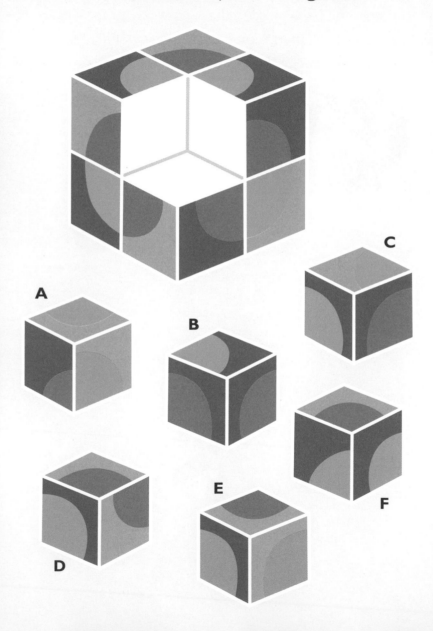

A

B

C

D

E

F

Funny farm

Circle the **six** things that are strange about this scene.

Reading the signs

Chief Running Bull has scratched this message on a
piece of tree bark. Use the signs on the opposite page to
see what it means.

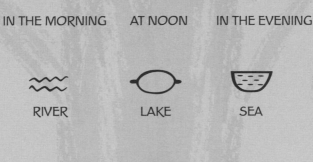

IN THE MORNING   AT NOON   IN THE EVENING

RIVER   LAKE   SEA

ROAD   FOOD   VILLAGE

TO DISCUSS   FAMILY   MEETING

ELDERS   WAR   FAR

NEAR   BRING   TAKE

River route

Find the right trail to guide the boat to the shore, avoiding the rocks.

Lasso display

Where should the rope be at stage 6 of this cowboy's
lasso display? Draw the rope in the cowboy's hands.

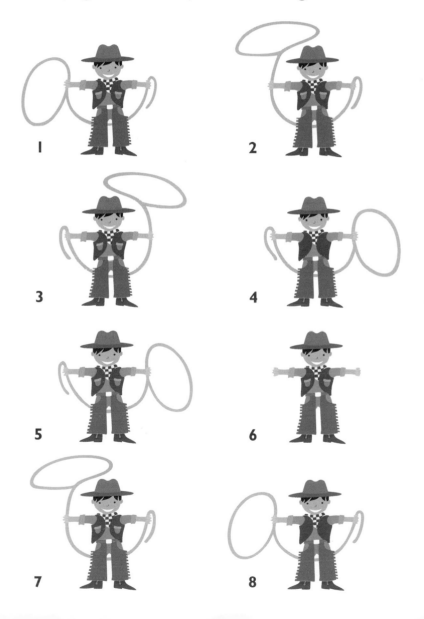

1

2

3

4

5

6

7

8

Who lives where?

1. Draw a line under Adam's house, which is immediately to the left of the house that is two houses to the right of the house that is three houses to the right of the house that is two houses to the left of the house that is immediately to the right of the purple house.

2. Circle Eve's house, which is two houses to the right of the house that is two houses to the right of the house that is immediately to the left of the house that is four houses to the right of the house that is immediately to the left of the orange house.

Picnic at the park

Circle the **five** things below that **wouldn't** be useful on an activity-packed picnic at the park on a sunny day.

Short shoelace

Draw a line along the shortest shoelace.

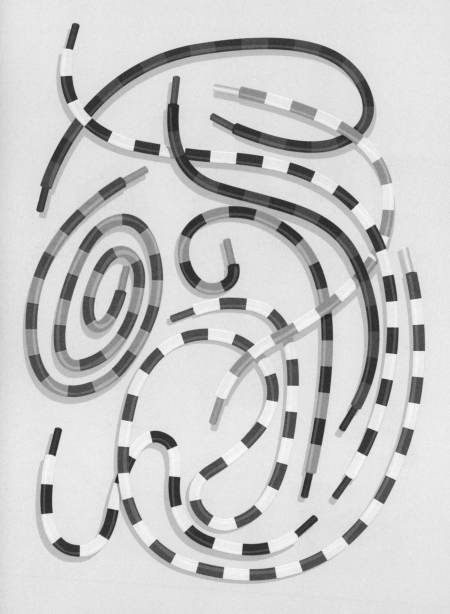

The way home

Alvok the Alien is lost. He asks three other aliens for directions back to his home planet.

Blinkon tells him:

"Go right at the red star, take the second trail on the left. Turn right, then, when you pass the green planet, take the first trail on the right. This will lead you home."

Marval says:

"Blinkon's wrong. Go left at the red star, then take the second trail on the right. When you pass the moon, turn left, then right. Follow this trail to lead you home."

Bluto says:

"They're both wrong. All you have to do is go left at the red star, then turn right. Follow this trail to lead you home."

Turn the page to follow the routes, then draw a line under the alien who gave Alvok the correct directions.

The way home

Look at the previous page to find out how to do this puzzle.

Growing order

Write the numbers of these pictures from a butterfly's life in the order they should appear.

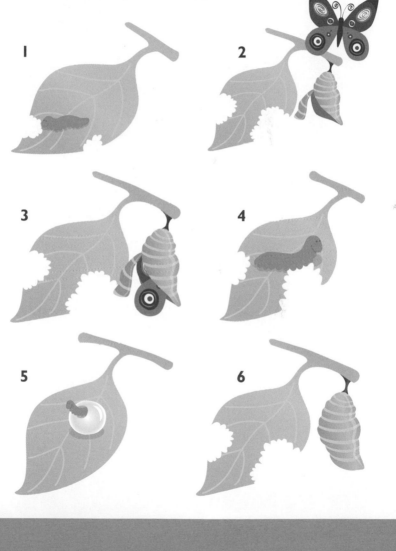

Answer: ....

Farm jumble

Look at the picture of jumbled shapes below and find the animals that you might see on a farm. How many are there?

Dotty ship

Join the dots in number order to complete the picture.

Bug spotting

Use the book below to find out what the big bug on the opposite page will eat. Underline the correct answer:

flowers / dragonfly / ant / caterpillar

► *Rainbow bug*

Rests on grass stalks, chews flowers.

◄ *Bright bug*

Lives near water, preys on dragonflies.

► *Striped bug*

Comes out at sunset, devours ants.

◄ *Motley bug*

Seen near mountains, feeds on caterpillars.

Hidden pattern

This pattern has been turned
around and hidden in the
block below. Can you find it
and draw around it?

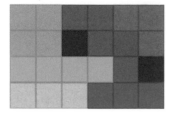

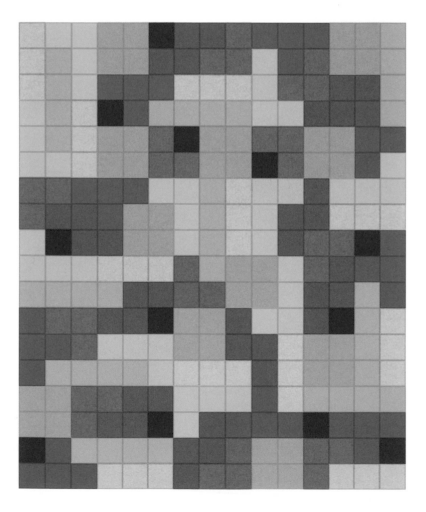

Hats off

Follow the trails to find out which skier dropped which hat, then write their names above their hats.

Animal prints

Draw arrows to join each animal to its correct covering.

Shape puzzle

Fill in the shapes that have blue dots. What can you see?

Crowd scene

Study this scene, then compare it with the one on the right.

Circle **six** differences in this scene.

Sandcastles

These pictures have become jumbled up. Write the letters in the order the pictures should appear.

Answer: ....

Spider's web

Help this mother spider reach the middle of her web without walking over any of her babies.

Diamond counting

How many diamond shapes are in this pattern?

Answer:..

Family photos

Memorize the people in these photographs for 30 seconds, then turn the page and draw lines to connect each pair.

Family photos

Look at the previous page to find out how to do this puzzle.

Patchwork quilt

Draw around the patches in the quilt that **haven't** come from the rolls of material at the bottom of the page.

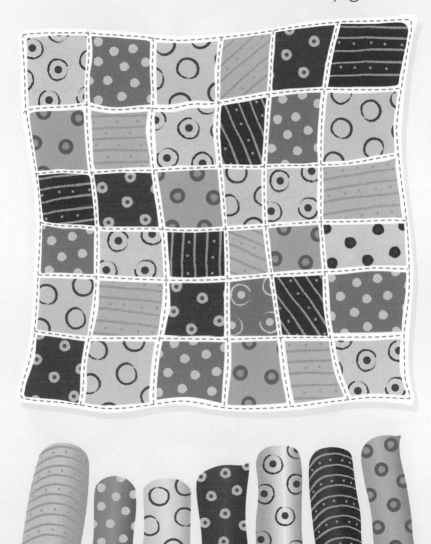

Rattlesnakes

Which rattle belongs to which snake?

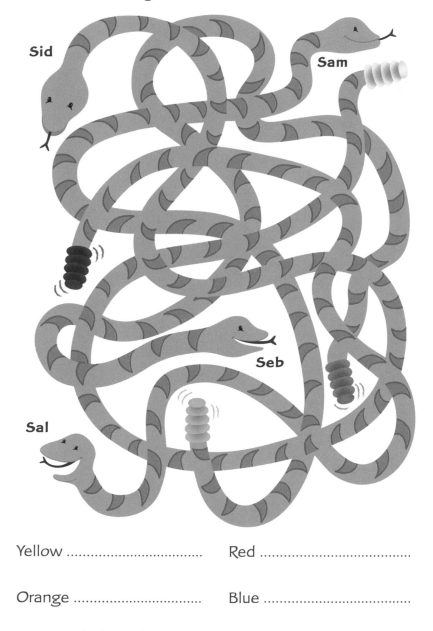

Yellow ....

Orange ....

Red ....

Blue ....

Watering hole

Count the number of zebras, lions and so on in this scene.
Then, turn the page to find out what to do next.

Watering hole

Look at the previous page to find out how to do this puzzle. Then, turn back and read the question below.

There's an extra animal in this scene. What is it?

Answer: ....

Odd bug out

Circle the odd bug out.

Egyptian error

Can you circle the **six** things that didn't exist in Ancient Egyptian times?

Dalmatian twins

Circle the two dalmatians that are exactly the same.

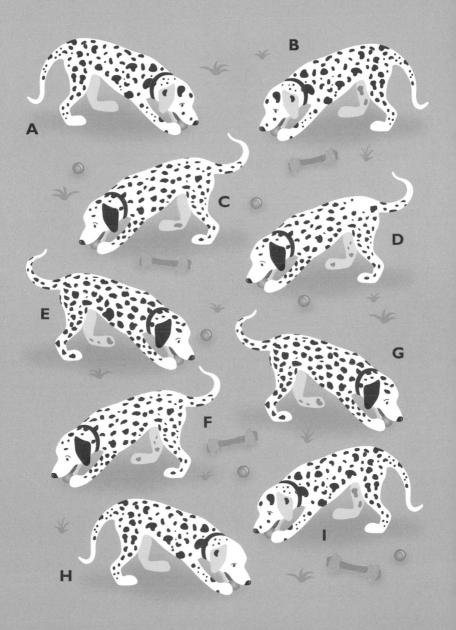

Going underground

How many of each of these things are in this picture?

coins........................

ants........................

worms........................

gems........................

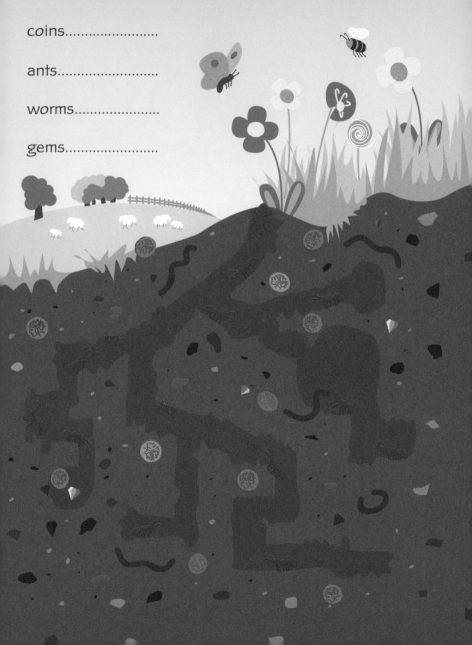

Counting cars

This pictogram represents the cars that drove along a road in a five-minute period. Look at the pictogram for one minute, then turn the page and follow the instructions at the bottom.

Key: 🚗 = 1 car

Counting cars

Look at the previous page, then turn back and follow the instructions at the bottom.

A

B

C

D

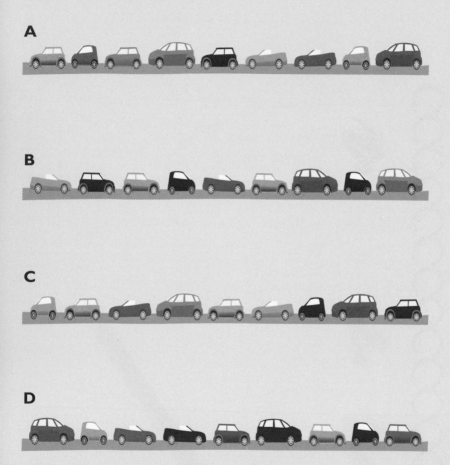

Without looking back at the previous page, underline the stretch of road that is represented by the pictogram.

Hidden picture

Fill in the shapes that have blue dots. What can you see?

Odd pair

Circle the two gloves that **don't** make a matching pair.

Puffin grid

Can you find these four squares in the picture below?

Bead brain-teaser

Following the sequence, draw the beads onto string E
in the correct order.

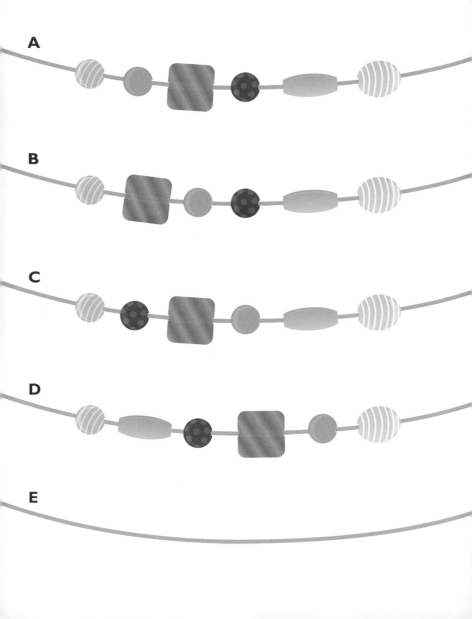

Busy bees

Follow the trails to find out which bee has visited which flower, then write the number of their flower under their names.

Pinboard pictures

These pictures have become jumbled up. Write the letters in the order the pictures should appear.

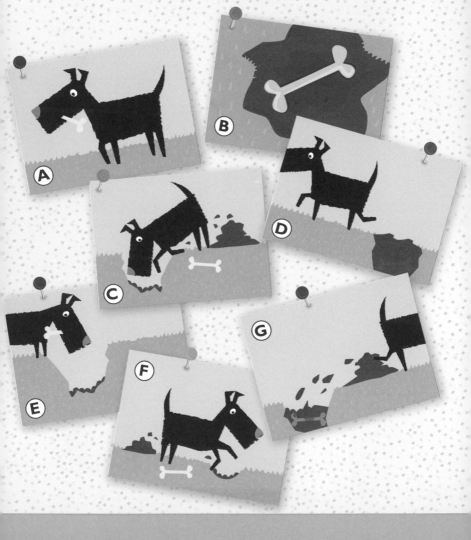

Answer:...

Memory mobile

Kate is out shopping when she gets a text message from her mother. Spend 30 seconds memorizing the list of food she needs, then turn the page to see the things she buys. What has she forgotten?

Memory mobile

Look at the previous page to find out how to do this puzzle.

Answer: ....

Jungle dots

Join the numbered dots in number order, then join the
lettered dots in alphabetical order to finish the picture.

Answers

1. Martian match

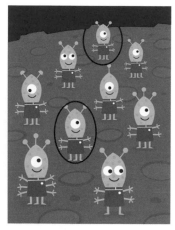

2. True or false?:
1.T 2.T 3.F 4.F

3. Which map?: B

4. Russian dolls

5. Dotty dinosaur

6. Planet maze

7. Birdwatching: Long bill

8. Camping count: 49

9. Block printing: E and B

10. Clothesline

11. Crocodile crossing

Answers

12. Food symmetry

13. Stamp selecting

14. Cupcake challenge

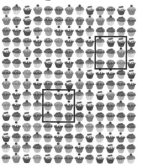

15. Going bananas: 8

16. Gift wrap: C

17. Sailing boats

18. Spot the circles

19. Making masks

Answers

20. Robot match

21. Mad scientist's lab

22. Monsters in the dark: 8

23. Turning cogs: B and C

24. Skewer sequence

25. Tower reflection

26. Curious campsite

27. Pyramid explorer

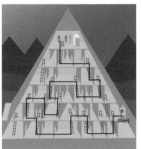

Answers

28. Fairground search

29. Shifting shadows

30. Musical jumble: 12

31. Hidden picture

32. Snail trails: Swirl

33. Shadowy waters:
A5, B6, C14, D8, E15, F13, G2, H4, I9, J3, K1, L10, M7, N12, O11

34. Robot reflection

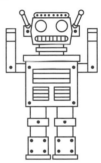

35. Medieval mistake

Answers

36. Matching sets: 5

37. Shape search: 22

38. Something strange

39. The right tools:
Screwdriver

40. Picture match

41. Monster mirror: F

42. Alien jigsaw: A and D

43. Odd one out:
1. bird; 2. tractor; 3. bear;
4. cactus

44. Truck parts: E

45. Switching seats

46. Naughty kittens:
Patch – 2; Misty – 3, Leo – 1

47. Complete the cube: E

48. Funny farm

49. Reading the signs:
MEETING NEAR LAKE AT
NOON TO DISCUSS WAR
BRING ELDERS

50. River route

51. Lasso display

52. Who lives where?:
1. Adam – blue house
2. Eve – pink house

53. Picnic at the park

54. Short shoelace

55. The way home

56. Growing order:
5, 1, 4, 6, 3, 2

Answers

57. Farm jumble: 8

58. Dotty ship

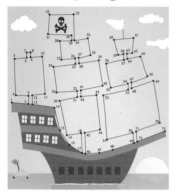

59. Bug spotting:
dragonfly

60. Hidden pattern

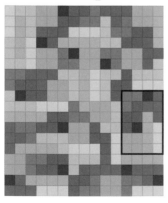

61. Hats off:
Orange hat – Enzo;
Green hat – Dan; Blue hat – Gia

62. Animal prints

63. Shape puzzle

64. Crowd scene

Answers

65. Sandcastles:

E, G, B, F, H, A, C, D

66. Spider's web

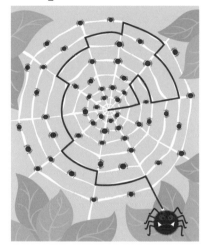

67. Diamond counting: 35

68. Family photos

69. Patchwork quilt

70. Rattlesnakes:

Yellow – Sid; Red – Sal,
Orange – Seb; Blue – Sam

71. Watering hole: Giraffe

72. Odd bug out

73. Egyptian error

Answers

74. Dalmatian twins:
B and I

75. Going underground:
11 coins; 14 ants; 5 worms,
8 gems

76. Counting cars: D

77. Hidden picture

78. Odd pair

79. Puffin grid: C6, J4,
F5, F12

80. Bead brain-teaser

81. Busy bees:
Barney – 1; Bertie – 3;
Beatrice – 2

82. Pinboard pictures:
A,F,C,E,B,G,D

83. Memory mobile:
Lettuce

84. Jungle dots

Written by Sarah Khan
Designed by Joanne Kirkby, Ruth Russell and Candice Whatmore
Illustrated by Lizzie Barber, Non Figg et al.